Tibet Summit
Reflections On Tibet And The World

EARLIER WORKS

Konsten att vara Lycklig, 1989,1991
Tibetanska Talspråket, 2001
A Simple Guideline on Tibetan Buddhism, 2002
Från Lidande till Lycka, 2009
From Suffering to Happiness, 2013

OTHER WORKS FROM SVENSK-TIBETANSKA SKOL- OCH KULTURFÖRENINGEN

Att Hitta Hem, 2000
The Jewels of Tibet -- A Rosary of 108 Schools, 2006
Den Sanna Frihetens Väg, 2010
Sagor Från Tibet, 2015

Svensk-tibetanska Skol- och Kulturföreningen, The Swedish-Tibetan Society For School And Culture, is a politically and religoiusly independent organisation. The primary purpose is to build and operate schools i Tibet and to create a cultural bridge between Sweden and Tibet.

Tibet Summit

Reflections On Tibet And The World

Soenam T. Jamyangling

Svensk-tibetanska Skol- och Kulturföreningen, 2018

Cover photo: By I, Luca Galuzzi, CC BY-SA 2.5, https://commons.wikimedia.org/w/index.php?curid=1810976

ISBN 978-91-9814-331-7

Original blog administrator: Tenzing Jamyangling

Layout and book production: Stig Jonsson, digitalamedia.eu

Print: BoD – Books on Demand, Norderstedt, Germany, 2018

Dedication

We are living in a world burning with fire, instead of creating a heaven here on earth. This 21st century is a critical stage for mankind when we will either create a society where we all can live peacefully in harmony, or create a place where we are going to experience extreme hell. We cannot expect God, Allah, or Buddhas to sort out our mess around us. We created it and we must clean it up.

I hope this Tibet Summit will bring hope and dialogue between people and countries and that it will bring realization for the readers that our earth itself is a beautiful heaven. Therefore we cannot allow it to be destroyed by a few crazy and selfish people. We all are protectors of this earth which is our home and we must protect it for the sake of the many generations yet to appear.

Contents

III. Environmental Issues   65

Introduction

At the age of six, I entered a Buddhist monastery in Tibet. It was in 1959, when the Chinese Red Army invaded\ liberated Tibet, that I was sent with one of my uncles to escape over the Himalayan mountains to India. Thanks to the Danish Tibet Committee, headed by Prince Peter and Mr. Fenneberg, I had the opportunity to study in Denmark and later was offered a scholarship to study in Tehran, Iran at the Polytechnical Institute.

After receiving my diploma, I was one of the first Tibetan technicians, educated in the west, and had the opportunity to serve in a Tibetan refugee settlement in southern India. It was there I married a Tibetan woman, whom I had earlier met in Denmark. We had three children, although two of them were taken away from us due to smallpox and meningitis. Our surviving daughter now lives in Boston. In 1971 I returned to Denmark and from there traveled to Sweden, where I worked at a Buddhist center for 17 years, remarried and had a son. My third and last marriage to Anne-Sofie took place in Lhasa in 1998. She became my wife and trustworthy life long friend.

It was in 1988 however, when I decided to create something concrete in hopes of benefiting the Tibetan people. That year I had the opportunity to return to Tibet for the first time in 29 years to see my father. It was then that I learned that my dear mother had been tortured and killed by the Red Guards. In 1993, after five years of negotiations with the local government, I was able to start the first humanitarian aid project in Tibet. The first project was to build a school in my home village of Katsel. After its completion, I have been back to Tibet many times, and in 2006 we celebrated the completion of our goal – to build 108 schools and 108 libraries. Currently our schools consist of over 13,000 children, all who depend on our help.

If we really want to, we can all develop for the better – as it is not only something that monks and nuns have the opportunity to do. I learned that it is our own doubt that is our biggest enemy. It was only when I stopped having doubts, that schools were built and our goal was achieved.

Stockholm August 24, 2017
Soenam Jamyangling

CHAPTER ONE

Education & Health

Educational and Cultural Project from Sweden

"Education costs money, but then so does ignorance"
-Sir Claus Moser

"Education's purpose is to replace an empty mind with an open one"
-Malcolm Forbes

I hold dearly that education is a key to wish fulfilling gems. In this point in time, without an education, life often is clearly more difficult to live. Therefore it was with my aim and determination that many friends from all over the world took an interest in education in Tibet. It has become clear to us that with education, the Tibetan people can develop their own country with the help of others such as China and other nations. We also realized that the best gift to share with one another is education with the right attitude. With a clear frame of mind and determination, we were able to build 108 schools and 108 libraries within Tibet in cooperation with the local people of the areas as well as the Chinese authorities both inland and abroad.

We are proud to announce to the world that now more than 250 students who have graduated from our schools are now studying in highschools and universities both in Lhasa and China, and that 13,000 children are studying in our 108 schools. With the help of our old and new sponsors, our project can continue to make a difference in Tibet.

Although Tibet has changed harmoniously, Tibet still needs help in global development. That way mainland China does not need to support Tibet economically forever.

If you are interested in our projects in Tibet and would like to support this meaningful mission, please contact us. When you sponsor a Tibetan child, you are helping to develop Tibet as well.

April 3, 2009

HIV/Aids project in Tibet

Society in Sweden was very happy and satisfied for the co-operation that they had with Lhasa and the various Local Authorities in Tibet. Their staffs in Tibet were so lucky that they could implement the project and be able to co-operate with the local people and their various Authorities there. Without co-operation with the Chinese and local people in Tibet, they could never have done it alone, therefore I would really like to express here my gratitude for the TAR leaders for understanding of the very important mission.

I knew that there was no HIV/Aids at all yet in Tibet, but was very necessary to educate the masses in Tibet. There were many men, women, young and old from different districts, who attended the training and education about the disease.

As I have said it before it seemed the project went on well and the Swedish Tibetan Society for School and Culture could at least be able to introduce to the people of Tibet, the prevention technique and some knowledge around the HIV/Aids. The Lhasa Authority and leaders of the other districts in Tibet appreciated the best gift from Sweden, the training and workshop on HIV/Aids.

The TAR television showed the whole programme on CCTV and it even reached Nepal, China and India. People in Nepal and India were very surprised that they could see such a useful programme on HIV/ Aids from Tibet and that it was supported by the STSSC from Sweden.

On behalf of the people of Tibet I am forwarding their gratitude to Forum Syd, Sweden and the leaders of the Swedish Tibetan Society for School and Culture in Sweden. I hope the STSSC will continue 2009 similar programme in cooperation with Lhasa Authority and other part of the China. Recently the Swedish Tibetan Society for School and Culture completed HIV/Aids project in Tibet for 2006-2007.

May 1, 2009

Visit from Beijing

On 22nd June the STSSC received a delegation from Beijing headed by Professor Hao Shiyuan, Director of the Institute of Ethnology & Anthropology, Chinese Academy of Social Sciences.

The other members of the delegation were:

* Mr. Tanzen Lhundup. Associate Professor of the Institute of Sociology & Economics, China Tibetology Research Center.
* Mr. Dawa Cairen. Associate Professor of the Institute of Religion, China Tibetology Research center.
* Ms. Wang Yanwen (Tashi Tsomo). Vice Division Chief, China State Council Information Office.
* Mr. Gao Ming. Interpreter/attache, Ministry of Foreign Affairs, P.R.C.
* Also present at the visit were representatives from the P.R.C.'s Embassy in Stockholm.
* Both STSSC's board members and the guests had the opportunity for a very meaningful dialogue during the visit.

July 4, 2009

MEETING WITH THE DALAI LAMA

Q 1. We have completed 108 schools in Tibet, so now what more?

D.L. Every effort made in Tibet is very important. Continue with all your efforts. You can do it here too.

We have a difficult political situation, but that situation is changing from within China. More and more intellectuals show sympathy and concern for Tibet. The official Chinese view is expressed by officials, but in private communication some such persons express understanding. So, there is no reason to feel discouraged. Do not feel discouraged! My feeling, after all that I am hearing from businessmen and artists for example, is that there is a keen interest inside China for Tibetan culture. As an example of this, in Beijing these days there was an arts exhibition by artists. Tibetan culture was mentioned with interest.

The general Chinese population knows very little about Tibet. They also know very little about the very big differences between Tibetan and HAN perspectives. Yet more and more the Chinese recognize Tibet and are interested in Tibet, and there is some positive changes among the Chinese businessmen. You in the Swedish Board should try to find forms to have dialogues with Chinese. It makes your work a little easier. Your attitude should be frank and transparent. We are not always in agreement with the Chinese point of view. But we emphasize and agree with what the Chinese constitution states in terms of ".. all people should get better education". The Tibetan language is different from the Chinese. Thus the Tibetan language (not only vocal but also in script) should be used for this education task – not Swedish or Chinese!

I have met top scientists from USA and Germany several times. They are eager to learn from Buddhist science. In my view we can talk about 3 different aspects of what Buddha taught: a. Science b. Philosophy c. Religion

So far the Science of Matter has nowadays been developed the most. The Science of Mind is urgently in need to be developed. These western scientists need for example to develop the science dealing with destructive emotions. A key issue is: what to preserve from the earlier type of knowledge? The Tibetan style of approaching life is not always aggressive like the Khampas! I myself come from Amdo. We are a different sort, and he (Soenam) is from U (Central Tibet).

Q 2. Tibet is changing so rapidly. Would H.H. not like to co-operate as quickly as possible with the PRC?

D.L. The question relates to the entirety of Tibet, not only part of it. The United Front often accuses us that we drive the issue of 'Greater Tibet', which are not words that we use. Here they refer not only to the Autonomous Region, TAR, but also to areas under Tibetan influence, such as the 4 other provinces. The issue is: how should we treat all these areas? Even the Prime Minister has recognized Tibetan interest not only in TAR, but also in the 4 other parts of Tibetan related regions. Today the Chinese government accepts this view that you have to consider all these regions when speaking about Tibetan issues. Some western scholars told us that we are asking for too much! But we do not understand 'independence', (nor claim for independence for these areas) in the same way that the Chinese do. Rather, we consider this issue to be closely related to what is within the Chinese constitution, and of its implementation and regional connotations.

At this moment the United Front always demonstrates a negative attitude, so we can wait. But we are also ready to participate in discussions and negotiations, especially with the constantly renewed Chinese government and leaders.

In the meantime, your organization seems to be doing a very good job with the PRC. Good Luck to you! Don't you have any issues with the Chinese? The Tibetan spirit is very highly strong!

Q 3. We have been purposely friendly with the PRC and have been able to set up our school system for 13,000 children. But can our small organization play a minor role in facilitating a dialogue between Beijing and Dharamsala?

D.L. No! They – the Chinese – do not want to have any 'go-betweens' as far as we have understood it.

Q 4. Would H.H. not like to visit Tibet to see the transformations for himself?

D.L. As early as 1983 we took the initiative and expressed our interest that I wanted to go to Tibet. We even planned for the journey. The Chinese government refused the visit. In 1992 again a new attempt was made. In the 4th meeting the United Front offered that I could send some observers to check the developments in China. With regard to me coming to China (not to Tibet as was my proposal) they said that the Dalai Lama cannot come, not even as a spiritual person as we had suggested. He (the Dalai Lama) would always come with his political role, they said. So there was no travel at that time either. But I am ready to go there if their approaches change.

Q 5. Aside from psychological support – what kind of practical assistance do you and the 'Exile Government' extend to Tibetans living in Tibet?

D.L. Nothing! As an expression of the deadlocked situation I will provide a recent example. When the earthquake occurred recently in China I sent some money to the Chinese, but they rejected the support. The Chinese are refusing all help from the

Dalai Lama. I also sent money to the Pakistan Embassy after their earthquake. First they accepted it, but then sent the money back. Inside Tibet, the Chinese reject any funds coming from the Dalai Lama. So at this time we cannot operate at all inside Tibet.

Q 6. Is there any special department within the 'Exile Government' designed only for the Tibetan cause?
D.L. There is no separate, specific department for internal or external matters.
In our administration here it concerns dealing with those who come from Tibet, in terms of education or rehabilitation needs, and in organizing the Reception Center for refugees both in India and Nepal.

Q 7. Should a group of people not be set up who can give a clear picture of what is going on and in this way promote a better understanding and atmosphere for the dialogue with the PRC?
D.L. I think the obstacle before was ignorance, but now nothing can be done because since 2008 the Chinese know what is going on here. The present leading administration in Beijing decided that the Dalai Lama should not be allowed to visit China or Tibet because then they think that the problem will get worse.

A Chinese person told me that when in Lhasa he had seen an old Tibetan woman doing prostrations in front of the Jokhang temple. Just beside her there were Chinese soldiers doing military exercise and yelling at each other. The Chinese person felt that it was as if they were doing this intentionally to provoke the lady. Actually, they are the real 'splitters'. They think that Tibetans will give way under the pressure of the gun. Nowadays more and more Tibetans have negative feelings towards this method. One thing that can help for example is that more than 1,000 articles have been written in Chinese showing the truth about the situation. I always say that the power of the truth is more powerful than the power of the gun.

So, we must have more contact with businessmen, artists, etc. It is no longer any use to keep in contact with the politicians. We meet officials and businessmen and we know that outwardly they criticize the Dalai Lama, but then they have my photo in their pockets! One should have more contact with Chinese visitors in order to provide a new and true perspective for them.

Q 8. It is sometimes said that if change is to come, it must come from inside Tibet. What kind of change is it you are waiting for and expecting to happen in Tibet?

D.L. First, the Tibetan national spirit is there! That holds true for both uneducated and educated alike. And it holds true for the religiously minded and for those who are not so religious. Those who are more sensible in Tibet fully support our approach. Writers and educated Tibetans are supportive of the middle path that we have introduced before. For the time being we do not expect some new ideas or change, or new events. After 2008, 99% have a strong national spirit which is much sharper than before. The Chinese look at every Tibetan with suspicion.

Q 9. Your Holiness has often said that education is the key and it is the most important factor for the development of Tibet. What kind of support in the field of education has the 'Exile Government' been able to extend to those living in Tibet?

D.L. Nothing! The only thing I have been able to do is to ask some NGOs to support students coming from Tibet and to give them the means for their education. But this has been outside of Tibet. This has been very useful.

Q 10. We have heard that the 'Exile Government' has chosen 'Regional Autonomy' for all Tibetans, a long process! Are there not some short cuts and a quicker solution for Tibet (e.g. in terms of the autonomy of Central Tibet)?

D.L. Ironically, the simplest way to approach this problem would be if I, after fifty-one years of struggle, was to give up one day, and to move on that day singlehandedly to China with a white flag of surrender in my hand. But the Tibetan spirit is very firm so I cannot give in. Never give up! Never! In the short term we do not envisage any great changes. In early 1980 something seemed to happen as the Chinese leader Hu Yaobang was in Lhasa. He said at that time that 80% of all complaints from Tibetans were mostly true and that there was a strong need for new openness. Very soon after, a 5-point program was launched by the Chinese authorities about what to do. But then suddenly there was no movement any longer.

A Western journalist recently asked me what I would like to ask his Prime Minister. I answered that a Prime Minister does of course have influence, especially in the government, but that others in society such as businessmen and professors etc. are also independently very active, for example in the field of education. So, it is not always government leaders that are the keys to the development, especially not if they are arrogant! Ordinary people can be much more important.

I would like that people abroad take every chance to inform Chinese who are passing through their country about Tibet. Information coming for example from Chinese, who have been abroad, would carry more weight.

Instead of criticism of Chinese behavior, one should focus on the importance for China, in a modern world, to create more trust by developing in accordance with their (Chinese) constitution. The current lack of openness is very harmful for the Chinese development. They should be recommended to open up their society.

December 10, 2010

CAN WE FIND A PEARL IN THE SHIT?
THE ANSWER IS, YES

The Times of India, dated December 15, 2010.

There was an interesting article on "Self Is Pure Consciousness" by Anandmurti Gurumaa.

While I was reading world politics with all the intrigues I saw this wonderful article on our true Self. I want to share this blessing to friends and request you to kindly put a little time for yourselves, to examine and meditate on your consciousness in these times around the end of the year and beginning of the New Year 2011.

Here the article that was written in The Times of India.

Self Is Pure Consciousness. Your true self is the purest of pure. It is the witness. Even if you are not aware of the self, it will not lose its identity. But when identification of the Self happens with the body and mind then the self is in a state of delusion makes you suffer.

Self is Sakshi, Pure Witness. However, you need to be aware of this. To be truly happy, you need to experience the Self. Then you come to understand that you are pure through Brahmngyan, pure knowledge, that you come to know about your own true Self.

Your body is constantly changing, through pure knowledge you could understand how many different bodies you have had and yet you are the very same existence, how many births you took and all those bodies died but you always remained untouched by death. You may not be able to recall one single body out of those thousands

of bodies that you took, but yet you are the same unchangeable purity.

Similarity, the mind too is in flux, it is always changing with plenty of good and bad thoughts lurking in the mind, all the time. Who knows all this? It is you and you alone who are witnessing these changes happening in body and mind continuously. The intellect too behaves differently, sometimes buddhi or intellect goes crazy and at other times it acts intelligently.

When I say that self is Sakshi Swaroop or Witness Incarnate, do you comprehend what I am saying? Knowing it with your mind is not enough, the experience has to be there, is that not strange: knowing and yet not knowing? Those who do not realise their Self, does their Self die with the body? No. Even the Self of ignorant people is immortal but they fear death due to their ignorance. However, the one who has realised purity of self simply laughs when he encounters death.

You are consciousness, pure existence and this body is mortal. The Self is pure existence and a witness. In Self-awareness there is immense joy and in not knowing the Self there is a lot pain and suffering.

The Self is chetna, superconsiousness, the one who knows, pure existence, truth, everconsious – satchitanand. That bliss will come to you only with experience. When would pain, suffering, jealousy and hatred take leave of your mind? This will happen only when you understand and realize that the mind also is different from you. No doubt it is close to you but still it is not you.

Be a witness. Remain detached. You just be watcher, a seer; be aloof from all this paraphernalia of the world and the body. Then only can you really enjoy otherwise you will suffer as no scenario is ever going to remain unchanged.

Change is bound to happen as it is the very nature of mind and this whole world. An enlightened being would say: If is birth that is fine if it is death that is also fine – as nothing can happen to the Self.

The realized ones would say: "What can death take away from me

– nothing! What can life give me – nothing! All the dramas of the world is happening in front of me.

Let it happen whatever has to happen, Therefore why worry."

January 23, 2011

A SMALL GIFT FROM ME TO YOU
from the Times of India (Friday January 28, 2011)

Of Strangers and Friends

By Maulana Wahiduddin Khan

"Normally preoccupied with family members and a small circle of friends, most of us do not generally want to become familiar with strangers; we look upon them as 'others'. This kind of thinking is based simply on suppositions about others — and sometimes such suppositions are unfounded Experience shows that it is perfectly possible to make friends out of strangers. Swami Rama Tirath, a man of considerable education, decided in the last decade of the nineteenth century to visit the USA, despite paucity of funds and not knowing anyone there who could receive him and host his stay there.

After a long sea voyage, he reached the American coast, where he disembarked along with the other passengers. There were many Americans who had come to receive their friends and relatives at the port. However, Swami Ram Tirath found himself walking all alone by a corner of the port. An American, seeing him there, approached him and asked,'Do you have any friends in America?' Swami Ram Tirath said:'Yes, there is one friend and that friend is here'. Saying this, he embraced the American. This kind of behaviour was unexpected and the American was impressed.

He said:'Yes, I am your friend' and then he took him along with him to his home. Swami Ram Tirath remained his guest till he left America for India. No one is a stranger to you; everyone is your potential friend. Just behave in a friendly way and accept others as your sisters and brothers. If you can sincerely adopt this kind of friendly attitude, you will find that everyone is your friend and no one is alien to you. The fact is that all the men and women have common ancestors. This means that the whole world is a single family and everyone has that kind of attachment with others that is so noticeable in family life.

It is only distance that makes you a stranger. If you eliminate distance, nature will prevail and all can be like blood brothers and sisters to you. The formula for friendship is very simple. If you are truly a friend to others, then you can safely predict that they will also become your friends. Develop genuine love for others in your heart and then others cannot but love you in return. A philosopher said that man keeps radiating feelings all the time. If you are a compassionate person and you are radiating compassion, then others are bound to receive those radiations of compassion from you.

If you have developed love for others, then you are radiating love and others are bound to receive the radiation of love. This is the law of nature. You will therefore receive a positive response to positive radiation and a negative response to negative radiation. The only condition in this regard is that you should be a selfless person. Positive behaviour combined with selflessness always works. It is selflessness that makes your behaviour ring true. On the contrary, if you are a selfish person, your behaviour will be like that of a salesman".

And such behaviour cannot have any positive effect. Abide by your own nature and you will be a successful person. Everyone is born like an angel, but after receiving negative impulses from his environment, he becomes otherwise. So, return to your original nature and you will be acceptable to all!

WE ARE WAITING FOR YOUR ACTION AND CONCERN 13.000 children who have dreams urgently need your support in Tibet:

The Swedish Tibetan Society for School and Culture (STSSC) remarkably completed 108 schools with 108 libraries in Tibet and now the most important project left is to support the 13.000 dreams of the children's future. We request and need your love and compassion in action to support them so that they can get a complete education.

There are now more than 1000 students who are attending higher studies and university education both in Tibet and the Mainland of China. The STSSC supports these children.

Without our economic support and concern these children have no future at all. Please kindly think *if you were in their situation* and share some funds monthly so that you can also feel good that you are helping another human being. They need your action now!

There are many ways to help, but to act with love is the highest support that we can share with each other.

The families of these children are very poor and cannot support the high studies and university educations in Tibet; therefore I request you on behalf of these children and their parents, please kindly extend your hands to support their education.

Without education there is no future for Tibet, and the children are our future!

Please contact to:
Swedish Tibetan Society for School and Culture,
Vivstavarvsvägen 200,
S-122 43 Enskede
Sweden
Telephone: +46-8-643 49 47 Telefax: +46-8-643 49 17.
Pg 900666-9
Internet: www.tibet-school.org, E-post: info@tibet-school.org

* Name & address of bank : SWEDBANK S-105 34 Stockholm
* Swift address : SWEDSESS
* Account holder : Swedish Tibetan Society for School & Culture
* Within European Union : IBAN Account no.SE0380000838164031120241
* Other countries: Account no.(Clearing 83816) 403.112.024-1

June 27, 2011

CHAPTER TWO

Political Dialogue

"Prisoner of the State: The Secret Journal of Premier Zhao Ziyang"

An extraordinary private version and political interpretation by the deceased Prime Minister of the PRC, Mr. Zhao Ziyang.

How often can we get information with this kind of impossible and unobtainable theme? Yet, Mr. Zhao Ziyang has made it possible for us to take a glimpse at the hidden backside of the great wall of the PRC! I got the unique opportunity from a friend to read this rare and strange book in Swedish, while lying in hospital. Otherwise I would neither have had the time nor the inclination. It turned out to be a strange and magical description of the most complicated, dark and powerful spiders – the web situation of a country. I was both shaken and confused at the same time. It was extremely complicated and difficult to understand the various political transactions that are going on in a country like China. But she gives the impression of running her show seemingly well and the rest of the world sharing in her delight. They show little doubt, but accept her as one of the leading super-power nations which has the possibility of transformation. In any case, China is developing slowly and carefully. But the sad thing is that there is a lack of mutual trust, and a huge gap between old party leaders and the newer, younger ones. They are now in some kind of bardo or "intermediate" state! For the welfare of the people and the country, the leaders of the PRC must find a good solution soon; so that we do not have to repeat the same kind of incident like the one that occurred on June 4th in the year 1989, with the world looking on.

A peaceful and harmonious dialogue is the best strategy for the future of mankind and also for the people of the PRC.

When you read this book, it seems that visibility is covered by dark confusion. Yet, at the same time there is also a strange penetration of light of goodness too. It seems that Deng Xiaoping and Zhao Ziyang had different approaches to the June 4th event in 1989. However, if you look very carefully you see that there are more actors involved. If you read this book, you will get tremendous insight into the PRC and it will be easier to understand the complex society. You can then make your own judgement instead of listening to the opinions of others.

April 5, 2009

60 YEARS FRIENDSHIP BETWEEN THE PEOPLE'S REPUBLIC OF CHINA AND SWEDEN

The Vice President of the PRC, Mr. Xi Jinping was invited to Gothenburg, the second biggest city in Sweden to celebrate 60 years of friendship between the two countries. Sweden has recognized the People's Republic of China since 1950. Mr. Xi Jinping gave a talk at the city hall for Swedish enterprises and met the Prime Minister of Sweden, Fredrik Reinfeldt, the Deputy Minister Maud Olofsson and other important politicians.

Mr. Xi Jinping witnessed the historical moment when Volvo PV and Geely Automobile, the Chinese automaker, signed the final agreement for the business transaction on Volvo's transformation. Then it was written in Dagens Nyheter, a daily newspaper in Sweden with the largest morning circulation, that the New World Order has come forward. Sweden is now China's largest trade partner in Northern Europe.

Mr. Xi Jinping was in Sweden for several days and visited many important institutions. Approximately four to five hundred Han Chinese and other minorities from other areas of China were invited to meet him. I was one of them and had a great opportunity to meet him. I presented myself by shaking hands with him and with the words "Tashi Delek". I was also able to present a book "The Jewels of Tibet" as well as a letter that says:

The reasons for building 108 schools in Tibet:
*   To support and develop culture and tradition through education

31

    *   If appropriate, according to the Chinese policy, I would like to facilitate and extend my help for a dialogue between Beijing and Dharamsala.

My sincere wish is that one day we all can be with our loved ones in Tibet-China.

It is extremely comfortable and beautiful abroad, but "home is where the heart is".

May 6, 2010

MR. BIRD NEST (AI WEI WEI)

Without Ai Wei Wei, what is the use of having a heavenly square in the middle of Beijing, and the bird nest that was created in a peaceful country where there are so many wonderful people who are living together in harmony.

A bird nest without birds, what is it? China, a nation that is rapidly going foreword and will hopefully be the leading nation in the world. But this kind of narrow-mindedness with funny thought processes deducts from her creativity and credibility as a leading nation in the world. What a shame!

I am a good friend of China and I am ashamed of this kind of news that appeared in the world news. It was shocking news and sad for China. Had Mr. Ai Wei Wei not worked as an artist and put time and heart for his country when he was needed at the time of the 2008 Olympics in Beijing?

He is a true citizen of China and he had the highest ranking artist title in his country and abroad. He was a well known artist in the world too. He does not deserve this kind of punishment and discriminating processes in a country which is slowly becoming the biggest and most powerful nation in the world. How can we let him deduct from the credibility of the Chinese Nation that is so slowly marching into a perfect harmony? We must ask questions concerning this matter.

This kind of small incident can lead to a bigger chain reaction and at last one cannot control it at all. Be careful! Do we need this kind of reaction? I hope this will not happen! Please stop this kind of unbalanced attitude toward him and instead take care of him with respect and love and treat him as the highest qualified artist in China. Can this be a good idea for China or not? It is up to the leaders and people of China… I leave it to them!

I have no idea what he has done wrong, but I know him as an exceptional artist in China and in the world. He was one of the creators of the bird nest. Sorry, this is my spontaneous reaction, if I have made a quick judgment on Ai Wei Wei, please forgive me.

Friends of Ai Wei Wei, how can we help Ai Wei Wei and China?!

July 17, 2011

DALAI LAMA AND US, WE TIBETANS

Do not expect what Tibetans can do for Dalai Lama,
but keep on expecting what Dalai Lama can do for the Tibetans!

This is one of the true issues of Tibetans at the present time. Tibetans do have faith and trust in Dalai Lama, but we do not contribute anything concrete to support his middle path or the non-violent movement. Rather, we support him through three ways:

1) Devotion and respect
2) Collecting offering money or things for his long life.
3) Attending his teachings.

These above three things have become so easy and so wonderful for the Tibetans that they do not do anything else. But then the big job is left to Dalai Lama. The question is, is it fair that only one man has do everything while the rest is having a party and making their life more and more rich? Most people think that when you meet Dalai Lama that all your problems are pacified and you are again a new fresh person. That is all well & good, but what about Dalai Lama and Tibetans in Tibet? When your big ego is satisfied when you meet Dalai Lama, do you then continue to support the Tibet issue or does it disappear when He is gone? Most of the people go to Him so that they can get blessings and purification.

The question is do we follow his teachings that were given to us concerning other human beings in this world every day? The answer is very doubtful! So what is the use of staging shows of those kinds of pretension again and again? At last it becomes like a big joke! Instead of carrying out his advices and putting his teaching into practise for the sake of others well being, you instead even disturb his dialogue with China by means of creating unnecessary activities.

Many times I felt we were cheating Dalai Lama and ourselves by being two-faced. That means, we are so devoted in front of Dalai Lama but as soon as we are away from him we do completely something else, and that is maybe a big reason why the Chinese refuse our request of autonomy for our people. I have a suggestion for you all. Please forget about collecting money for Dalai Lama, and instead, do as Dalai Lama told you to do. That will give him a very long life, we will be much happier, and at least in that way we might pay back his kindness. And, I believe, there will be a dialogue between Tibet and China too.

There are three things to remember from Dalai Lama:
* Our Chinese brothers and sisters.
* Within the framework of People's Republic of China.
* We Tibetans are neither anti-Chinese nor anti-China.

September 2, 2009

What was Ngapo Ngawang Jigme's Karma, the Cause and Effect?

When Reting Rinpoche was acting as the selector of the new Dalai Lama incarnation, Mr. Ngapo was there and he saw the changes in his Government and in the country. He was neither a devil nor a Buddha, but an intelligent man. Ngapo Ngawang Jigme was the son of a Tibetan aristocratic family descended from the former Kings of Tibet. After studying traditional Tibetan literature, he went to Britain for further education.

When he returned from Britain, he served in the Tibetan army and later in 1950 he was appointed governor (commissioner) of Chamdo, the third biggest city, but took charge of the office only first in September. Unfortunately he took responsibility at the wrong time, when there was tremendous confusion in the old Tibetan government. The Dalai Lama was young and all the decisions were made by Tadrak Rinpoche, the new regent and his ministers.

Mr. Ngapo Ngawang was dedicated to the former regent Reting Ripoche and he enjoyed working under him. Mr. Ngapo Ngawang was also very interested in the Nyingma Buddhist School as was the Reting Rinpoche. Defenders have alleged that Reting Rinpoche's imprisonment was partly the result of his attraction to the teaching of the Nyingma Lineage, a politically sensitive orientation, and that the case against him had been fabricated by the cabinet minister Kapshopa and others who had been hiding behind him.

All this nonsense was noted by Mr. Ngapo Ngawang Jigme and he made his decision to be part of the revolution or reform. He then agreed with China that as long as Tibet was going to have the so-called Tibet Autonomous Region for itself his plan would be to shape the country better than anyone else, with the help of Chairman Mao Tsetung. Then of course he signed the 17 point agreement without the Dalai Lama's and Tadrak Rinpoches's permission. This is the main issue that we are still struggling with China about today.

Whether Ngapo did right or wrong, he made a huge change in the old Tibet. His motivation was to reform Tibet with help from China and he believed in the 17 point agreement that he signed in China. He is at the same time the biggest reformer and traitor in our modern time for the sake of Tibetans living in Tibet.

As I mentioned, Ngapo Ngawang Jigme's motivation was good but he was there for us at the wrong time and perhaps in the wrong environment. Whether he was right or wrong, we had a huge and important Tibetan person with a brain who played such an important role in China:

Ngapo Ngawang Jigme's life:
1) Commander – in-chief of the Tibetan army forces at Chamdo
2) Head of the Tibetan Delegation to Beijing Peace Negotiations.
3) An advocate of reform
4) Implementing the Seventeen Point Agreement
5) Administrative, military and legislative responsible
6) Secretary General of the Preparatory Committee for the Tibet Autonomous Region
7) President of the Tibet Autonomous Region
8) President of the Standing Committee of the National People's Congress.
9) He was an honorary member of the "Buddhist Association" beginning of 1980
10) Honorary President of the Tibe an Wildlife Protection Association that was found in 1991
11) He was also the President of the China-Association
for the Preservation and development of Tibetan Culture,

which was established on June 21 2004.

Beijing announced that Ngapo Ngawang Jigme was a great patriot and good son of the Tibetan people, outstanding leader of China's ethnic work, and close friend of the CPC.

The exile Tibetan government headed by Prof. Samdong Rinpoche called him an "honest and patriotic person who made great effort to preserve and promote the Tibetan language". "He was someone who upheld the spirit of the Tibetan people". [nggtags gallery=0012,0013]

My own opinion is that he was an extremely outstanding and brave person, in the sense that he stood there between Beijing and Dharamsala for more than 50 years. He had contributed towards reformation in Tibet and he was head of many important organisations in China, and through those organisations he preserved and developed Tibetan culture and education as best as he could. Now he has passed away, but he left many interesting questions for us to solve.

Finally, I would like to express my sympathy that we have lost an important person from our lives. Yet, he left in our hand a gift of courage and energy for further development of reformation in Tibet.

Delek Shok!

February 2, 2010

CAN THIS BE AN ACCOUNT OF MONEY AND POLITICS OR IS IT A MEETING OF DOGS AND WOLVES?

Recently shocking news on the activities of the Shungden Society was revealed by a man named Tsering Tashi (Lama Tseta), who has been Chairman of the Shungden Organization. He is the first person to come out of their organization and spot-light their activities around the world. He is accusing his former friends of collaborating with communist China and of preparing to take the lives of many important people in the Tibetan community in India. He also exposed the danger for

HH Dalai Lama's life. Such accusations are very difficult to digest and seem almost impossible to believe but since it was shown on the YouTube "Boston Tibetan Truthful Public Talk" there must be some truth to it. Therefore I am sharing this unbelievable news with you all so that you can judge by yourself. The following is a summary of the program "TRUTH", the background of the worldwide demonstrations for Shungden.

Lama Tsetan comes from Lithang in Kham, in eastern Tibet. At an early age he entered Pomra Khangtsen at Sera Mey Monastery in India. In 1997 he was appointed as one of the four officials for the Shungden Committee at his monastery. In 1999 he was appointed Chairman of the regional Shungden Society by the Shungden Oracle and through this he came into stronger contact with the Shungden movement. He says that he does not have faith in Shungden and he clearly knows that Shungden is a fake and cannot go into trance. China always tells the Shugden propitiators that the Dalai Lamas from the 1st to 13th were not enemies, neither of China nor Tibet, but that the 14th Dalai Lama is the common enemy and that they must work together in confronting him. There are lots of accusations from Lama Tsetan and his friends. It is an interesting subject and very useful. By exposing who is behind the Shungden movement he has put his own life at risk. I therefore think it is worthwhile to see "TRUTH" and come to your own conclusion. The two sides have their own stories of course. Below are lists of people mentioned by Lama Tsetan in the recording:

The group who helped Lama Tsetan to expose the movement consists of the following people:

1. Thintey Kalsang
2. Ngawang Chime
3. Thupten Thkmay
4. Dhamchoe Nyima
5. Lobsang Ngodup

The group who is involved in the Shungden Society consists of the following:

1. Geshe Kesang in England
2. Gangchen in Ital
3. Nga Lama/leader
4. Dragom Rinpoche
5. Tenzin Palchok
6. Thupten Phurbu (Head of Shungden in China)
7. Gonsar in Switzerland
8. Ngagpo Gyatso
9. Dechen Tulku
10. Athar Tsering
11. Konchok Gyaltsen/ leader
12. Chatreng Yeshi/leader
13. Choezay/ leader

The people from the United Front are:

1. Zhu Weiqun
2. Sithar from Derge
3. Lobsang Wangdu from Gyalthang
4. Various other names from Tibet and China

I could write a long article on this subject but I urge you to see the document-ary yourself and to make your own judgment since we are all living in the so-called free world. Finally, I recommend you all to see "TRUTH"… and to be watchful!

July 27, 2015

Who dare to accuse our great leader Mr. Lobsang Sangay?

Recently an article written by a woman named Maura Moynihan on Lobsang Sangay appeared in the Washington Times. When I first saw the article I could not believe what I was reading with my own eyes and I read it again and again several times. I was both sad and shocked at the same time. I therefore decided to inform you, my readers to read it and make your own judgment concerning the article. It contains very serious accusations and they must be answered by Lobsang Sangay himself. He can also bring up the case in the Parliament, where the peoples' representatives can interrogate the Prime Minister nicely concerning all the complicated issues it entails. As it has been said: "The H.H. the Dalai Lama's wish is for transparency in the Central Tibetan Administration."

I do hope this case can be solved as soon as possible, so that the people of Tibet do not need to feel ashamed of their own Prime Minister.

Here is the link to the article:

http://www.washingtontimes.com/news/2015/jul/10/maura-moynihan-tibet-china-same-washington-lobbyis/

There is an old saying in Tibet:

"If there is evil inside, nothing can be achieved on the outside" So please solve this issue first before you do anything for Tibet!

August 18,2015

The win-win policy of the Chinese President

On September 24- 25, 2015, Xi Jinping visited Washington and he brought with him the win-win business policy to buy 300 Boeings from the United State. Xi said that the Boeings were a "win-win example in Sino-US relations". Xi showed this time that he is not only the President of PRC but that he is also a damn good businessman! The 300 airplanes list prices put the deal's total value at

US$38 billion.

The American leaders were indeed so happy with the business deal, that the Human Rights issues in China, Xinjiang and Tibet disappeared almost completely from the ears and eyes of the American citizens. Again, I must say, Xi Jinping did it well. He showed that even on American soil he is the leading leader of the New World Order, as did even his wife.

The President of the United States acknowledged again that Tibet is recognized by them as part of China, but that China must improve the Human Rights issues in Tibet. But by starting with this recognition statement, that Tibet is part of China, the President of the United States then has no longer any right to involve in the internal matters of China. And thus the whole topic of Tibet became like delicious food… but without any salt in it!

November 4, 2015

MISSING

Missing for 20 years Yes, that's 20 years now UN!

A boy named Gedun Choekyi Nyima, vanished 24th May 1995, He was one of the youngest political prisoners in the world, Do you have any ideas of how he is, or of his whereabouts, UN?

Missing for 20 years. Yes, that's 20 years now UN!

We called him the 1th Panchen Lama, Do you perhaps know where he is, Or what he did that was so wrong? Or did Tibetans not fight well enough on his behalf, UN?

Missing for 20 years Yes, that's 20 years now UN!

What about that then, UN? Where is UN when he really needs you? Are you all afraid of the super-powers, UN? Or do you all just only think about your own future?

Missing for 20 years Yes, that's 20 years now UN!

In the 20 years that followed since the 6 year old child disappeared, UN, you did a few things, but not with heart nor dedication, Minor things accompanied by major "blah, blah, blah"s, then more "blah blah"s. This child has been calling for your help to release him from his jail so many years!

Missing for 20 years Yes, that's 20 years now UN!

UNITED NATIONS, you must be strong, an organization with integrity based on love and compassion. Fight for justice in

this cruel world and in particular for our Human Rights. There are injustices in every corner of the world. There we all need you, UN!

Missing for 20 years Yes, that's 20 years now UN!

Please free the Panchen Lama at once from house arrest, At the age of six he went into that prison! How can you let this happen to him, UN? He was so young and innocent and has surely done no wrong, If you UN cannot help him, then please tell him where to go,

Missing for 20 years Yes, that's 20 years now UN!

Please show your true face now UN and free the Panchen Lama, (Or would you rather choose to side with 'them'?) The young Panchen Lama still has a strong faith in you, unlike us UN, So, please kindly act now and act truthfully without 'agenda' and 'protocol'. We, the citizens of the world and the young Panchen Lama await your answer.

December 9, 2015

At last the wisdom eye of UN opened

It took around 60 years until UN got a man who really will fight for justice in the world in the name of Human Rights issues, without any distractions cause by economic reasons or fame. Thanks you UN and other nations, for you have found the right man for the right job. I and many other friends have lost hope for the UN, but now hopefully my trust in them will slowly grow again. It is not only the question of Tibet, there are many nations and individuals in the world that have the same problems like in Tibet. But many times it is difficult to detect the situation in good time. Therefore we need many honest professionals, like as I mentioned, and like in the following article:

Phayul, on August 24, 2016. UN envoy criticizes China on human rights, interference in work:

The United Nations human rights representative yesterday criticized the Chinese government for the 'drastically' shrinking space for human rights in the most populous country in the world and for interfering with his work during a China visit. Philip Alston, the UN Special Rapporteur on extreme poverty and human rights, at the press conference in Beijing after 9-day official visit to China, complained of drastically shrinking space for civil society actions to discuss government policies.

"None of those meeting were arranged, and the message I got from many of the people I contacted was that they had been advised that they should be on vacation at the time", said the Professor at NYU School of Law.

He also shared that he was followed everywhere by the Chinese officials and an activist who was trying to get a meeting with him was detained near the UN office in Beijing.

September 10, 2016

WHY XI SMILES AT MAO?

After reading many articles on Xi Jinping in various newspapers I find it difficult to understand their speculations about him. I therefore allow myself to share with you my own ideas here, but the absolute truth is somewhere in between all the speculations. Fifty years on, China found this leader who is a product of the Cultural Revolution and who spent fifteen years in a cave. His father was a wartime hero, but was subjected to public humiliation, struggle sessions and repeated beatings because of Mao. Of course Xi smiles at Mao, because now he is the most powerful leader of the whole of China and maybe he will be more powerful than all the leaders together, including Mao. Many people speculate that Xi Jinping will follow in Mao's footsteps, but in my opinion that will never happen. He might however use some of Mao's methods Xi is not as unsophisticated as Mao. He is also cleverer but will use some of the methods of Mao in order to build a China that will be the most powerful nation in the world. His ambitions are enormous and when judging him we might make mistakes between Xi and Mao. They are two completely different types of leaders. And besides, we

are now living in the 21st century; therefore we must understand the quality of leadership and what his aims and objects are. Around Mao's time China was isolated and so he could do anything with his people, such as killing two million Chinese during the Culture Revolution, while the rest of the world was busy with something else. Times have changed and so has leadership. Xi has more responsibility about China globally because of the bilateral relations with other nations and so it is too early to conclude that XI Jinping is transforming into Mao.

We all know politics is a dirty game; therefore we must all use our imagination with common sense so that we are not deluded by wrong information from newspapers, internet and other media.

Let us wait and see – the time will tell. "Your patience with wisdom reveals the truth at last".

May 23, 2016

Could this be a final Good Bye to Tibet?

In the Hindustan Times it stated: "China to build second railway link from Lhasa in Tibet".

This means maybe that Tibetans have lost their beloved country forever, so now it is no use to fight against China.

Can't you imagine what China can do when they built the second railway?

Tibet will not be same as before and the Chinese will have

one hundred percent control over Tibet and the countries that exist in the Himalaya hemisphere. China is a nation that will proceed with their plans day and night until they complete their objectives, while the rest of the other nations are lost in their democratic debates and differences. The Chinese did it in the past and she will without a doubt do it again. When they have completed building so many railways from many directions in Tibet, that will also be the time when China got the whole of Asia right in the palm of their hand.

From the Hindustan Times: "China will build a second railway line connecting remote Tibet with the southern part of the country, expanding connectivity and increasing its options for rapidly moving troops to the area".

As we can see very clearly, the Chinese activities are very concrete and aggressive and it is really happening. So therefore, what kind of strategy could the CTA have to challenge it? They cannot kill any more time expecting that other nations will provide support for their struggles. Now it is time to wake up and do something! Create a strategy with concrete plans that will challenge China and forget about trying to fight against China with so many words. The fight using the word is almost over, so do you not have any other suggestions left with which to obtain your country back?

Stop expecting support from other nations, but expect more from yourselves, with an excellent planned strategy. You cannot do something again and again (such as 10th March demonstrations) that has not given you maximum satisfaction, but now instead you can bring new suggestions for your people to bring the Chinese to the negotiation table. If you do not have any fresh method and means to fight or to settle the differences between the Chinese and Tibetans, then we cannot keep on doing same old things again and again.Either let the Chinese rule Tibet forever or hurry up… the time is running out!

May 23, 2016

THE LEADERS FROM TAIWAN/CHINA HOLD AN HISTORIC MEETING

Two gentlemen, Mr. Xi Jinping and Mr. Ma Ying-jeou met in Singapore. The meeting was an historical event for there has not been any communication between the mainland China and Taiwan for 60 years. Saturday 07-11-2015 will be the historical foundation and bridge-day between the two countries and also between the two leaders. They are brave and intelligent beings who have really created an open-minded policy which can bring goodness to two countries for many generations yet to come. We must admire their bravery and their example and we hope that the two countries' citizens can have more peaceful and harmonious relations in the near future.

Written in China Morning Post: "In the future whoever is elected the president of the Republic of China – Taiwan can continue to use this platform to advance cross-strait relations."

Well, this kind of story also brings hope and understanding for the China–Tibet relations. This can bring inspiration for both sides so they can finally find an everlasting solution for their issues.

If China wants to solve the Tibet issue, then start with the Dalai Lama while he is still alive, otherwise the Tibet case will bring so much pain and suffering for both sides.

Nothing is impossible. When the windows of possibility are open on one side, one should take the opportunity to open one's own.

Good luck to China and Tibet!

February 22, 2016

Tibet has been completely changed

During the last 28 years time, there has been changes going on nonstop in development in the whole of Tibet. Changes are good if you want to develop Tibet and it is good for both the Chinese and Tibetans. Since we started our educational project in Tibet there has been lots of changes that went on and those changes were partly to prevent foreign aids and foreign influences. It was very interesting to study the Chinese Government policy on education and the development scheme in Tibet. Their whole project schemes were to have hundred percent control of Tibet from the Dalai Lama and the Central Tibetan Administration, and from foreign influences The Chinese main goal is to make maximum profit from the natural resources of the country, such as from the Himalayan mountains, forests, rivers, etc.

I do not recognize my birth place. It is completely transformed into a Chinese city and people are forced to adjust to the Chinese way of life and my people are suffocating from these types of developments. But the whole world is neglecting this beautiful country of Tibet because of the Chinese exaggeration of their goodness and the so-called peaceful liberation of Tibet under gunpoint.

Tibet and the Tibetan people are dying slowly due to lack of freedom of speech, movement and expression. Tibet is isolated from the rest of world by huge mountain chains and these mountains, with which the Chinese policy in Tibet created the artificial so called wonderful heavenly Tibet, is now transformed into a hell. The Chinese already built one railway from China to Tibet and there are creating another one soon. This means that we, the citizens of this world, have silently helped and supported the Chinese policy to kill and root out the Tibetan culture and people from this world, because we were kept quiet and blinded by the Chinese fancy words and money. Remember, Tibet is the head of the mother earth and she holds all those major rivers of Asia. If she goes with China completely, then slowly one by one all the countries in Asia will face drastic consequences and the eco system of the environment will slowly but surely show another change of face. The question of Tibet is to do with whole world, therefore take necessary peaceful actions wherever you are and whenever you have time. I really do worry about the future of the whole world, not only Tibet. Tibet is a tiny part of it, but Tibet plays a very important role in the ecosystem.

Generally the Chinese people are very nice, but the one sided policy of China must be synchronized for the welfare of the Tibetan people and for mother earth as well. China must respect and listen to the Tibetans living in Tibet. They should not bulldoze down the Tibetan culture as the Chinese like to do. There is a saying: When you are China, do as the Chinese do… and that same thing applies to the Chinese. When you are in Tibet, do as the Tibetans do, not the opposite of it.

If you both sides follow this simple rule, then there will be peace and friendship between the two nations and their many nationalities.

October 13, 2016

Asia Paper, July 2013

I read and studied the so-called Military Transformation with Chinese Characteristics in the New Century. The paper is divided into seven aspects:

1. Executive Summary
2. Introduction
3. The Context for China's Military Transformation
4. The Content of China's Military Transformation
5. Challenges Facing China's Military Transformation
6. Conclusion
7. About the Author

There is no doubt that China's Military Transformation is expanding rapidly and sooner or later she will be the most powerer nation on earth. When I go through the summary of the paper it explains in the short twenty sentences the whole idea of transformation as follows:

> *"The development of the worldwide Revolution in Military Affairs provide China with a rare historical opportunity, but also with unprecedented challenges. Seizing the opportunity and accelerating the military transformation with Chinese characteristics*

is a prerequisite for China's efforts to build a moderately prosperous society. After more than ten years of steady gradual reform, China's national defense and army building has achieved a new historic level of development. However, the task of military transformation with Chinese characteristics is still complicated, involving all aspects of national defense and army building. After the Eighteenth National Congress of the Communist Party of China in 2012, the next steps in military reform with Chinese characteristics and the principle, priorities, and goals of development were further defined. Although military transformation with Chinese characteristics has a long way to go and many challenges lie ahead, with the further deepening of reforms, integrity in the modern Chinese military system and revolutionary reform will ultimately be accomplished. Once achieved, China will make a greater contribution to stability in the region and also to world Peace and development".

When China transforms into a military super power then there will be a new world-order and the world will be definitely divided into two sections:
   a) Can create a kind of World Peace under military direction
   b) Catastrophe and destruction that lead to a third world war

Nevertheless, no matter whatever is going to happen, we should hope for the best. It is difficult to believe that military power alone can create genuine world Peace. Let us hope this will not instead create more challenges and confusion worldwide, even starting the third world war. Should we not have learned more by now from what is happening around us today by using modern mass-destructive weapons?

We cannot run away from the truth of what has happened in Afghanistan, Vietnam, Iraq, Syria, and other countries. War goes on with weapons!

We can only hope the China's military transformation with Chinese characteristic can include some of the human touch that is called love and compassion. Without it everything else will be useless. What worries me most is that there will be more challengers to the Chinese's Military Affairs and if that happens the world will be in a hell.

So I would like to ask my readers: what is your reaction to this article? Hopefully you can bring some constructive suggestions to those who believe that weapons will bring World Peace. Can this not be an illusion, cheating ourselves again and again?

Hopefully the Chinese will learn more from our present history of the Super Powers of the World and their deeds and actions….. that resulted in mass starvation and millions of people becoming homeless.

June 22, 2015

THEY DID IT AGAIN!

A so-called Forum, held in the autonomous region's capital Lhasa, hosted around 100 delegates from various parts of the world. They had a two-day forum on the development of Tibet on August 12, 2014. This forum was co-sponsored by the Information Office of China's State Council and the regional government of Tibet. The forum sought to gather opportunities and suggestions for Tibet's future. The protection of the Tibetan culture and environment was also to be highlighted.

It seems to me that we now can just take it easy, because the whole world is going to be involved in the Tibet issue and they will hopefully shape up Tibet through "leap-frog development." So, it seems also that Dharamsala has nothing to do in Tibet since those 100 delegates will take care of Tibet from now on. Or do they have any comments on this issue? I would like to express my sincere good luck to those delegates who attended the forum.

Among the delegates from Britain, India, the United States, Africa and other countries "collective experience was pooled to discuss development strategies for the region." The question is why outsiders were there in the first place? Whatever happened to the " internal matters" we have so often heard mentioned in

the past?

In any case, this is the first of this kind of project ever welcomed by the PRC. I think that we should appreciate such a fresh and courageous initiative from the PRC to bring together people from different parts of world to discuss the future of Tibet at such forum. I hope this forum will bring development with peace and harmony in our society without any more self-emulations, and an increase in freedom of speech and movement in the whole of China.

January 18, 2015

IS IT NOT TOO LATE FOR AN AUTONOMOUS, FREE TIBET?

Geographically Tibet is isolated from the rest of the world and in the past the mountains were like a huge fence between the outside world. Now, 60 years later there are more Chinese living in Tibet and they control everything there. Yet we are still fighting for something that is almost like a dream. The Chinese Government will never let go of Tibet, for she has everything that China does not have. Therefore I ask to our people: what are the alternatives and options still left for us there so that we can achieve relief from our nightmares?

Do not dream on and on, on a story based on an onion-like truth on Tibet; having layers and layers, but eventually leaving no result in the end. Instead, bring concrete solutions and proposals for the Chinese Government and solve two countries most

complicated political issues. We are still dreaming on that other countries will support our wish fulfilling dream. But these countries have their own agendas with China. So, the time has come to think and plan very carefully and then talk to the Chinese. Only the Chinese leaders and our own people can solve the Tibet issue, no one else. So stop having expectations that others will help us in our cause and maybe better to expect more from ourselves and work hard to achieve our goals.

It seems to me that this fight now going on is a fight over many generations, and if that is the case we must inform our people clearly what kind of fight is going on. We cannot get Tibet back with the present policy, because the present policy is completely irrelevant for the Chinese. So we must find out soon exactly what is relevant for both sides, otherwise it will soon be too late for anything.

A precious 60 years has past and we are still dwelling in foreign countries and we are becoming old and our children will do the same unless we come with reasonable and relevant proposals concerning our beloved country and the loved ones in Tibet. Many of our families are there and waiting for us, so how long are we going to stay abroad? Many of our Tibet friends are helping and supporting our causes, which is excellent and we should be grateful to them. But the real fight of Tibet is ours and it needs motivation, dedication and hard work from the Tibetans living both in and outside Tibet. Only then we can achieve our goal.

Otherwise we will have to wait for a long, long time.

October 13, 2014

Beijing 2014

First of all I would like to ask my readers if you had a wonderful summer holiday. I hope you had quality time wherever you are.

In June 2014 I was in Beijing for a week. I had a wonderful time in Beijing where I met many old friends and our students who are studying at various universities there. On Monday June 30th there was an interesting article in the Global Times: In a speech by Mr. Xi there is maybe some hope/openness and perhaps changes are on the way.

Keynote speech focuses on worldwide cooperation and equal coexistence, by President Xi.

The following article was in the Global times "Xi calls for global approach to security":

On Saturday Chinese President Xi Jinping called on countries to participate in global security on an equal footing, saying that flexing military muscle only reveals lack of moral grounds or vision, rather than reflecting one's strength.

Xi made the remarks in a keynote speech at a commemoration marking the 60th anniversary of the Five Principles of Peaceful Coexistence at the Great Hall of the People in Beijing.

Stressing that security should be universal, Xi said that all countries have the right to participate in international and regional security affairs on an equal footing and that they should shoulder the shared responsibility to maintain security both internationally and in various regions.

"We should champion common, comprehensive, cooperative and sustainable security, and respect and ensure every country's security", Xi told an audience of over 700. "It is unacceptable to have security just for one country or some countries while leaving the rest insecure, and still less should one be allowed to seek the so called 'absolute security' of oneself at the expense of others' security," he said.

He called on countries to step up cooperation at the global and regional levels and jointly counter non-traditional security threats,

*fight against terrorism in all forms and remove the breeding
grounds of terrorism.*

*Disputes and differences between countries should be resolved
through dialogue, consultation and peaceful means, Xi said,
adding that countries should settle disputes and promote security
through dialogue.*

*"Willful threats or use of force should be rejected," said Xi.
"Flexing military muscles only reveals the lack of moral ground or
vision rather than reflecting one's strength."*

*He said security can be solid and enduring only if it is based on
a moral high ground and vision.*

*"We should work for a new architecture of Asia-Pacific security
cooperation that is open, transparent and equality-based, and
bring all countries together in a common endeavor to maintain
peace in the world," XI said.*

*Myanmar President U Thein Sein and Indian Vice President
Mohammad Hamid Ansari participated in the commemoration
ceremony and delivered speeches.*

*Also present at the commemoration were Chinese Premier Li Keq-
iang, top legislator Zhang Dejiang and top political advisor Yu
Zhengsheng.*

*In 1954, leaders of China, India and Myanmar initiated the
Five Principles of Peaceful Coexistence, which stand for mutual
respect for sovereignty and territorial integrity, mutual non-aggres-
sion, non-interference in each other's internal affairs, equality and
mutual benefit, and peaceful coexistence.*

*Xi also warned against attempts to establish a dominant civiliza-
tion in the world and said diversity of civilization is a defining
feature of human society.*

*"There are 7 billion people of more than 2,500 ethnic groups
who live in over 200 countries and 5,000 languages", said the
Chinese leader, adding that different nations and civilizations are
rich in diversity and have their own distinct features. "No one is
superior or inferior to others, " he said.*

*"We should respect diversity of civilization and promote ex-
changes, dialogue, peaceful and harmonious coexistence," Xi noted,
adding that human history has proved that any attempt to establish
a dominant civilization in the world is an illusion.*

September 2, 2014

WAS THE GATE OF DIALOGUE CLOSED
A LONG TIME AGO?

Yet the sayings and dreams still go on from one generation
to the next:

"The Chinese enjoy being suspicious and Tibetans enjoy being hopeful with expectations". These two worst scenarios
are completely opposite from each other and yet we have these
two extreme ideologies trying to solve the question of Tibet. Having these two kinds of scenarios, that are attached to their respective traditions and culture, we cannot solve the issues of Tibet
and China. It is just too complicated. These nightmares will keep
on forever until there appears a third extreme ideology or system
that will maybe bring liberation for both sides. We have heard the
same kind of mantras, which I am mentioning here, from both
sides for so many years now and it still keeps on.

On November 6, 2013, the Gu-Chu-Sum (former Tibet political
prisoner's organization) mentioned the following in the Phayul.com:
"Chinese white paper accuses the exile Tibetan spiritual leader,
the Dalai Lama, and his "clique" of separatist activities to sabo-
tage Tibet's development and stability. The paper adds that the
true aim of the Dalai Lama is to rock the foundation that has

57

ensured development and progress in Tibet".

With hopes and expectations, Tibetans living in exile keep on with this same mantra year after year, and the result can be worked out as easy as 3 + 3 = 6. That is all….and there will be nothing more to it!

Here is one example from the exile Tibetans: "..condemned the Chinese recent white paper titled `development and prog-

ress of Tibet and Human Rights issues´.. " This kind of mantra recitation has been done many times in the past and now it still keeps on like a powerful mantra from the exile Tibetan side, even though no one listens to them. The world follows after where there is fun and god (MONEY).

Put a stop to suspicions and expectations and instead create something new that will bring maximum result for both sides. Cut off the old traditions and attachments to your instable ideologies and bring something new and fresh to the world. We are ashamed of both sides in this world where everything stays still like the prayer flags that have no wind energy, unable to protect the environment from various `pollutions´. The dream world of both sides is on the verge of becoming almost destroyed… and you are left living in a horrible nightmare.

April 26, 2014

WHAT A SURPRISE AND HOW SAD THAT HEAVEN WAS HIT AGAIN!

It seems to me that everything is possible, when men set their hearts on something. Be aware!

There have been countless protests and demonstrations at the Gate of Heavenly Peace Square (Tiananmen) in Beijing, but it seems to me that the heavenly beings did not sense at all what has happened around the square. But when Twin Towers in New York were hit it was the biggest and the loudest news of all in this century. I just wonder what is really happening in today´s world?! What are the differences between the China and the United State of America and their respective citizens?

It was 4 June 1988 when a far-reaching student demonstration was organized at the Tiananmen Square, but it did not give maximum result. Instead, so many innocent young men and women lost their lives. Now again 25 years later, on 28 October 2013, Beijing was hit by a huge fire and so many innocent human beings again were killed, even the great Mao Zedong's picture almost gone with the flames. How can we recognize the Heavenly Peaceful Square as such, when so many wonderful young people were killed and died there? How can ordinary Chinese tolerate this kind of act? Unfortunately, before this recent incident at the Tiananmen so many young Tibetans self-immolated for the sake of their rights, but nothing has happened to solve their problems and struggles. What is really happening in China?

We the free citizens of the world, must we not request to the leaders of People's Republic of China and their citizens to bring a harmonious and permanent solution for their citizens, so that the great name given to square can again be restored to the Gate of Heavenly Peace Square (Tiananmen Square). I hope there will be peace and harmony in China, so that all the Chinese can enjoy this short live fully, and so that we can too, since we all are connected. We must learn to look at the bigger picture and focus on the next generations.

February 2, 2014

What is China?

China is a nation with a rich cultural heritage & modernization with millions of people living there. There are many millions of human beings that have various cultures, traditions, religions and languages that are living in this huge country.

The question is, are they all enjoying the freedoms of the various cultures, traditions, religions and languages? The answer is that it is doubtful, but they all are enjoying the modernization and the development.

China is a powerful nation and she is slowly becoming the only super power in the world. How did China become the nation it is now? Many Chinese went abroad to study and now many of them returned and are building up their country that was once under Mao Zedong's iron-hand control. But some thanks goes to Deng Xiaoping, who introduced the open policy for the Chinese.

This, in cooperation with foreign investments, allowed China to slowly and carefully build up the country to what it is today. China cannot develop the country alone so successfully without foreign investments. Due to foreign investments China is now globally important and connected with all the investments in the world. So Tibetans must learn and find a good solution with China to solve their differences, otherwise we are against the world.

What I mean is, China is in the world and the world is in

China. The world economy and politics is more complicated than back in the 60`s. I think we must find a better and more useful solution for China and Tibet, otherwise it will be like in Syria and Arab countries. If that happens it will be unfortunate for both sides!

October 14, 2013

WHAT ARE WE TARGETING?

When the world is rocking, must we not learn to target in on Tibet? Is our goal like shooting an arrow at a target in a dark room? No. I do not think so. I think our targets are the following:

To remember Tibet.
To think and dream about Tibet.
Visualize the smell of Tibet and her beautiful flowers that are growing on mountains, waiting for us.
Remember:
Tsampa and butter tea, the best food for us…
Our brothers, sisters and parents, who are waiting for us…
The mountains and rivers from the Himalayas, our life streams.
The beautiful blue clouds and cranes flying in the sky, our messengers.
Concentrating on going home (to Tibet) is our mission…
To build up your own country, instead of building houses and kingdoms in other countries which is not our mission.

61

Going home is our aim and objective.

Living abroad is good, but it is better to go back to Tibet when the day comes.

You are Tsampa-eaters and butter tea drinkers. You can never forget your country.

Did you really put your time and energy into building up your country? If not, then start now!

If you have the motivation to go home, you will do anything to get what you want.

You cannot put so much time into building up other countries, when we need your help.

You cannot blame the Chinese only, but learn to look at your own mind.

Ask yourself how much time and energy you are putting for Tibet?

If you want your country back, please concentrate and do things right!

It is no use that you just shout, only for INDEPENDENCE, when you have hardly any means to get it.

Common sense and hope is the only solution for our case.

To create a platform and to provide a facilitation can be useful for a dialogue.

October 2, 2013

Give & Take

Is it not all about give and take?

There have been ups and downs in the history of China and Tibet, but at last China got Tibet. The Chinese made huge developments in Tibet. There are airports, trains and modern roads and new buildings and bridges and so on. We need those changes in our country because the rest of the world is changing so rapidly. But all these questions about whether changes are good for Tibetans living in Tibet or not, we must ask the people who are living in Tibet. Only they can give an answer!

Nevertheless, now the Chinese Government has a strong iron-hand control on Tibet and they are telling and presenting to the World that they help in the development of Tibet through economic support and the infrastructure of the country. But the Chinese Government have never mentioned to the world so far, not even a word, that they take out precious Tibetan minerals, such as gold, lead, copper, iron, coal, water and also timber from Tibet.

The world witnessed that a huge gold and lead mine was hit buy an earthquake quite recently near the Lhasa area, a village called Gyama, where 80 people were killed. I and my party warned both Tibetans and the Chinese Environmental Department there when we visited Tibet in 1995-2006 that we think there will be this kind of catastrophe in many parts of Tibet in the near future. Of course, the Chinese must take things from Tibet otherwise where/ how can they get funds to develop Tibet? I do not think other parts of China will ever agree to share their income and resources for the development of Tibet alone! China is far away and therefore they can `exchange´ things with Tibet in this manner. They are not helping all the time.

I think the time has come for the new Chinese leaders that they announce truthfully that they make lots of income from Tibet and tell the world that Tibet is the Treasure Island of China. That is why China is there of course, not because of monks and nuns.

I hope the Chinese Government will demand tight security

and law and order around the mining in Tibet, so that everything will go smoothly with workers and hopefully there will be less destruction of the environment.

August 14, 2013

CHAPTER THREE

Environmental Issues

65

ENVIRONMENTAL CONDITIONS
ON THE ROOF OF WORLD

INTRODUCTION

For almost over three thousand years, Tibet with its three administrative regions, Do-toe, Do-med and U-Tsang existed as a sovereign nation. The communist Chinese took/liberated the country in 1949 and today China refers only to the so-called Tibet Autonomous Region (TAR) which they created in 1965 as "Tibet".

Tibet, commonly known as the "roof of the world" is situated at the very heart of Asia. It is one of the most environmentally strategic regions in the world. Tibet lies in the north of India, Nepal, Bhutan and Burma; west of China and south of East Turkistan. Covering a total area of 2.5 million sq. km., more than 2/3rd the size of India, it stretches some 2,500 km from west to east and 1,500 km from north to south. It has an average altitude of 3,650 metres above sea level and many of the peaks reach beyond 8000m, Mt Everest (Mt. Chomolungma), with 8,848m, being the world's tallest.

The Tibetan Plateau is the highest and largest plateau on earth and towers over the central part of the continent of Eurasia. It is bounded by the Himalayan mountain chain in the south, and connected with the Altyn Tagh and Gangkar Chogley Namgyal Mountains in the north. Its western part merges with the Karakoram mountains and its eastern part slopes downward more gradually with Minyak Gangkar and Khawakarpo Mountains in Yunnan.

Tibet was ecologically stable and conservation of the environment was an essential component of Tibetans' daily lives. Tibetans lived in harmony with nature guided by their Buddhist belief in the interdependence of both living and non-living elements of the earth. This belief is further strengthened by the Tibetan Buddhists traditional adherence to the principle of self-contentment, that the environment should be used to fulfil one's need and not greed.

With the changes of Tibet, this nature-friendly attitude of the Tibetan people was trampled upon by a consumerist and materialistic ideology. The transformation was followed by wide-spread environmental destruction in Tibet, resulting in deforestation, overgrazing, uncontrolled mining, and extinction of wildlife, waste dumping, soil erosion, landslides and other perils. The unprofessional companies continue to extract various natural resources without any environmental safeguard; as a result, Tibet is facing an environmental crisis.

ENVIRONMENTAL CONDITION

Tibet had the most successful system of environmental protection of any inhabited region in the modern world. Formal protection of wildlife and environment through parks and reserves were unnecessary as Tibetan Buddhism taught the people about the interdependence of all living and non-living elements of the earth. Buddhism prohibits the killing of animals and advocates loving compassion for living beings and the environment.

PLANTS: Over 100,000 species of higher plants used to grow in Tibet, many of them rare and endemic. The plant species also include about 2,000 varieties of medicinal plants used in the traditional medical systems of Tibet, China and India. Rhododendron, saffron, bottle-brush, high mountain rhubarb, Himalayan alpine scrofula, falconer tree and hell Bonne are among the many plants found in Tibet.

There are altogether 400 species of rhododendron on the Tibetan Plateau, which make up about 50 percent of the world's total species. According to Wu and Feng (1992), the Tibetan Plateau consisted of over 12,000 species of 1,500 genera of vascular plants, accounting for over half of the total genera found in China.

BIRDS: In Tibet, there are over 532 different species of birds in 57 families, which makes about 70.37 percent of the total families found in China. Some of them include stork, wild swan, Blyth's kingfisher, goose, duck, shorebird, raptor, brown chested jungle flycatcher, redstart, finch, grey-sided thrush, Przewalski's parrotbill, wagtail, chickadee, large-billed bush warbler, bearded vulture, woodpecker and beautiful nuthatch. The most famous and rare bird is the black-necked crane (trung trung kaynak in Tibetan).

WILD ANIMALS: The mountains and forests of Tibet were once home to a vast range of rare and endangered wild animals including the snow leopard, clouded leopard, lynx, Tibetan taken, Himalayan black bear, brown bear, wild yak (drong), blue sheep, musk deer, golden monkey, wild ass (Kyang), Tibetan gazelle, Himalayan mouse hare, Tibetan antelope, giant panda, red panda and others.

FOREST: Tibet's forests cover totalled 25.2 million hectares. Most forests grow on steep, isolated slopes of above 35 degree in the river valleys of Tibet's low lying south-eastern region. The principle types are tropical Montana and subtropical Montana coniferous forest, with evergreen spruce, fir, pine, larch, cypress, birch and oak among the main species.

Tibet's forests are primarily old growth, with trees over 200 years old. The average stock density is 272 cubic metres per hectare, but U-Tsang's old growth areas reach 2,300 cubic metres per hectare- the world's highest stock density for conifers.

MINERALS: Tibet also had rich and untapped mineral resources. It has deposits of about 126 different minerals accounting for a significant share of the entire world's reserves of gold, lithium, uranium, chromites, copper, borax and iron. Tibet has the largest high grade uranium deposit in the world. Amdo's oil fields produce over 1 million tons of crude oil per year.

RIVERS: Tibet is the source of many of the Asia's major rivers, including the Yarlung Tsangpo (Brahmaputra), Senge Khabab (Indus), the Langchen Khabab (Sutlej), the Macha Khabab (Karnali), Arun (Phongchu), the Gyalmo Ngulchu (Salween), the Zachu (Mekong), the Drichu (Yangtse) and Machu (Huang he or Yellow River), these rivers flow into China, India, Pakistan, Nepal, Bhutan, Bangladesh, Burma, Thailand, Vietnam, Laos and Cambodia. These rivers systems and their tributaries are the life-blood of millions of people in the continent of Asia.

WARNING:
More than 15,000 natural lakes are also found in Tibet and some of the prominent lakes are Tso Ngonpo (Kokonor lake) being the largest, Mapham Yumtso (Mansarovar), Namtso and Yamdrok Tso.

Our research figure shows that rivers originating from Tibet sustain the lives of 47% of the world population and 85% of the Asia's total population. Thus, the environmental issue of Tibet is not an inconsequential regional issue, but has huge global significance to warrant international attention. More than ever before, the need to save the Tibetan Plateau from ecological devastation is urgent. Because, it is not the question of the survival of Tibetans, but half of humanity is at stake.

April 3, 2009

Is the roof leaking?
(or, The forgotten Plateau of Tibet?!)

The good news from Xinhua and the BBC:

Tibet promotes Tourism expositions by the local industry to be held in mid-June, 2009.

– "The Xinhua News Agency 1 June, 2009 – the Tourism Bureau of Lhasa City and its subordinate agencies in Lhasa's districts and towns will attend two tourism expositions to be held in mid-June to promote the local Tourism industry."
– "It is also mentioned in Xinhua that the BBC will help to promote Lhasa's Tourism."
– "Beijing, May 25 (Xinhuanet) – the British Broadcasting corporation (BBC) has decided to broadcast a promotional commercial in December on its World Channel free to help promote Lhasa's tourism, according to Tibet Business Newspaper."

It is all well and good that citizens of the world can travel to Tibet and enjoy the magnificence of the country, but we also have a responsibility to be conscious about the environmental issues. Today in the world we are all very much concerned and involved in the climate changes and struggles against global warming and it sometimes seems to me as if the end of the world is here, but, what about the Plateau of Tibet, the roof of the world?
Well, if the roof of a house is leaking and falling apart, then the house will be in disorder. So too will the world that we are living in!

In Tibet there are many high mountains with glaciers and so many great rivers that originate from the Tibetan Plateau which sustain the lives of 47% of the world population and 85% of Asia's total population. Yet we hardly discuss climate changes and

environmental issues in Tibet in any of the world climate summits that are held in the world. Is it because the Plateau of Tibet is situated on another planet or have we been too selfish and one sided that we forgot all together that Tibet is existing at the corner of our world?

It seems to me that the world and the experts on sustainable environment issues have either a) forgotten about this mountain country called Tibet, or b) have decided to completely ignore that it exists, together with all of the questions surrounding it.

In any case, Tibet plays a very important role in connection with global warming and the issues of the climate changes in the world and she also plays a major role in Asia. The global warming issues in Tibet are the problems of the world, and therefore we must bring them up at the Copenhagen meeting on climate in December, 2009.

I do very much appreciate once again that the Tibet Plateau is going to be opened for all, but we must not forget to inform and educate all the tourists who will visit there from all over the world. All the tourists must take full responsibility to clean up after every step they take in the country and all the Tourist Bureaus in Tibet and the BBC must inform to all how important it is to be conscious about the sustainability of the environmental and about global warming issues.

From my own experience when I was in Tibet there are two kinds of tourist groups:

– Tourists from the west and other parts of the world who are educated in the field of environmental issue and global warming,

– Tourists (often domestic), who have less knowledge about climate and global warming problems in the world today.

It is most important to educate these tourist groups, so that they will not throw empty beer bottles and plastic bags and so on everywhere on the mountains and in rivers, etc.

My final request to all the Tourist Bureaus in the world and in Tibet and in the mainland China is: Please inform for all the tourists groups that they must keep the country clean and to take care of the Plateau of Tibet. It is not only for our sake, but also for our next generations to come.

June 12, 2009

Earthquake update

A big Thank You to all who have sent donations to our Society!

Our representative is now in the area and has used the donations for blankets, food & drink (mainly tsampa and butter, which they eat there) and clothes. We have received a report from him.

Among other things he writes: "Casualties are uncertain but there are around 4,000 dead. Every day they transport bodies to Sertha. So many people are homeless…many with children. Two areas worst hit are about 5km from here. There the houses were made of mud. Two monasteries have been badly damaged and more than fifty were killed. Now people have to live in tents and eat instant noodles.

" At present he is trying to make contacts with more suppliers in order to get more tsampa and butter. "

We need to plan food supplies properly, these people could be here in tents for up to a year" He was surprised to see that.." so many people have come quickly from surrounding areas and monasteries to help and work together with the aid-workers!".

The Chinese government has supplied tents, instant noodles and water. However, many of the aid-workers from mainland China were quickly struck by nausea and fatigue due to the high altitude.

In Tibet they are collecting money for the victims and the Society`s Handicraft School donated 10,000y.

April 22, 2010

The Power of the Zachu River (Mekong River)

Mekong = Zachu river runs from snow-covered mountains of the eastern Tibet Plateau and it is one of the most important rivers in Asia.

All major rivers in Asia originate from Tibet:

Yalung Tsangpo = Brahmaputra
Machu = Yellow river
Drichu = Yangtse
Senge Khabab = Indus
Phungchu = Arun
Gyalmo Nguchu = Salween (travels to Burma)

The Zachu River (Mekong River) runs from Tibet to the following countries:
* Thailand
* Burma
* China
* Vietnam
* Cambodia
* Thailand
* Laos

The Mekong is one of the world´s major rivers and the 12th longest. Often times, human beings living in those areas where rivers are, do not think very much about where the source of the river originates. It is usually thought about only when countries face various issues concerning the use of these rivers.

Recently there was an article in Svenska Dagbladet (SvD) newspaper, published on April 8th 2010 on the Mekong River. There was a huge issue about how the countries mentioned above will share the rivers. When I read the article, I felt so sad. There has never been any problems with the rivers during the many centuries when old Tibet/China existed until 1959. Nature has no boundaries. China's Tibet shared her resources like the river Zachu (Mekong) with all her neighboring countries without making any demands in return. They must learn to appreciate that.

All the rivers were allowed to be used by the citizens of the world, according to the Buddhist philosophy. Many of these rivers are holy to Hinduism, Buddhism, and other religions. Old Tibet had preserved and respected those rivers as the elixirs of life itself, for the benefit of the next generations to come. So our responsibility is to pass on that wisdom (bloodstream) to future generations. In this way the Zachu River redevelopment will be a sustainable development for the whole of Asia, and we can also prevent the destruction of fisheries, agriculture, hydropower and other environmental issues. Nowadays, we are so greedy that we would like to use all the resources for ourselves and not thinking about our brothers and sisters and their children in Asia. Please think about the future.

Here I would like to give a suggestion to all of the respective countries in Asia. That they must all travel to the source of the river (Tibet) and learn the sensitivity and
vulnerability of those rivers and then to discuss how we can share the rivers in the best way for a long time to come. I think it is a very good time for countries in Asia to wake up and see what is going on with environmental issues on the roof of the world.
It is never too late. Wake up now so you can do something concrete for your children, so that they will have a good decent life. They deserve it!

June 4, 2010

Earthquake hit in the western and eastern hemispheres of this same earth in 2010

The quake that hit in the west was more visible then the east. It was due to the information and exciting news around the whole activity that it was supported by superpowers and developed countries. Therefore the various help organisations jumped into this area that was hit by the catastrophe and supported tremendously them with immense material support which indeed was very good.

But the quake that hit in the east was completely forgotten by them. Therefore one sometimes wonders why we are doing this kind of injustice action? I do not find any reasonable answers to it. I have been asking myself, Is Tibet and China outside of this earth or on another planet? If it is, then it would be an acceptable answer. Otherwise it was very confusing for me, and others who lost their dear ones in the catastrophe. Are human values in the western hemisphere more precious then those in the east?

We were the only organisation that supported the earthquake areas in Tibet and no organisations wanted to help our people when they lost everything due to the earthquake which killed thousands of people. My question is, Are the people in Tibet less important human species than those who live in the west? Our organisations stretched our hands out for help and support from Swedish NGOs, but none of them responded to us. It was very sad to learn that when we really need their help they are not there at all!

We in the west believe in equality, the democratic system, freedom of movement and globalising, but how can we keep all those principals when we are not fair in sharing things in the same world that we live in?

SIDA, the Swedish International Development Co-operation Agency has supported one project in Apa (Ngapa) area. The second earth quake was completely ignored because of the catastrophe in the west which was apparently more important than the one in Tibet, which was very sad, indeed.

Some times SIDA and other help organisations follow the waves of the loud-speaker of the highest propagator of the trumpeting sound.

I hope that in the future they will search for the truth – the facts around the natural catastrophes in the world, and then act.

September 10, 2010

THE ZANGMU HYDROPOWER STATION IN GYACA COUNTY IN LHOKA, TIBET

Hindustan Times, New Delhi
Thursday, November 27, 2014

Last year the Chinese dam project has worried India as stated in the Hindustan Times. But what is the point of worrying when you do not do anything about it? India knows everything about what was going on, on the roof of the world, but she thinks that she has tolerance to wait and see what will happen up there, in Tibet. Tibet is not very far away from India, they have no time to wait if they would like to prevent an environmental catastrophe in India and neighboring countries, including China. India had better hurry up and act soon, otherwise after a few years it will be too late.

I knew already about dam building projects and mining procedures many years ago when our organization lead a delegation to China and Tibet and discussed issues concerning the sensitivity of
the environment. But no one listened to our appeals about the question of mining and building dams on the roof of the world. We care for the Chinese and Indians and neighboring countries of
Tibet. Because we know that climate changes are connected with dam buildings, mining and cutting down forests, etc. we had discussions on environment issues with the Minister of Environment in Beijing. They were very aware about it and were ready to do what they can, but since money is involved we were blinded my short time profit rather than a long time gain. Of course it is healthy to see that some hydropower stations are needed, but you cannot be so greedy that you control a whole eco system that was there from the beginning and switch to an artificial system that is against the laws of nature. Sooner or later nature will hit us back hard if do not be careful with the various elements up on the roof of the world. If the roof leaks then whole countries, people, nature, animals and neighboring countries will suffer immensely. This will be such a painful nightmare… and we will not be able to repair it back to normal.

"GREEN EXPERTS UNSURE OF ZANGMU´S IMPACT BY RAHUL KARMAKAR"

"GUWAHATI: Experts are not sure how a series of Chinese mega dams on Yarlung Zangbo – which flows into Arunachal Pradesh as Siang and meets two others to become Brahmaputra in Assam – would impact the Northeast." Arunachal Pradesh had in 2001 experienced unprecedented devastation after an artificial dam on on the river, presumably created by landslides beyond the border in Tibet, gave way. Reports from Beijing on the commissioning of the 540 MW Zangmu dam have rekindled the fears. "China says Zangmu is run – of –the river, a type of dam that technically has a limited impact area. The extent of downstream damage can be gauged from certain parameters such as dam height and how far it is from the border. One dam might not be dangerous but the real threat would be after all the dams start operation and release excess water simultaneously", Partha Jyoti Das, Guwahati-based water resource specialist, said.

The whole of Tibet is like a natural water dam and it has never been transformed into artificial dams until today. Therefore, must we not now be extremely cautious with whatever future plans that we might have concerning this? Rivers in Tibet belong to all the countries in Asia that coexist with China; India, Bhutan and Nepal, etc. Therefore China and India must have a meeting with all the countries in Asia to settle the usage of rivers of the Himalaya.

May 17,2015

MORE ARTICLES ONLINE:
WWW.TIBETSUMMIT.COM